The Improved Binoculars

The Improved Binoculars

Irving Layton

The Porcupine's Quill, Inc.

CATALOGUING IN PUBLICATION DATA

Layton, Irving, 1912-
  The improved binoculars

Poems.
Rev. ed.
ISBN 0-88984-101-2

I. Title.

PS8523.A98156 1991   C811'.54   C89-095338-4
PR9199.3.L39156 1991

Published by The Porcupine's Quill, Inc., 68 Main Street,
Erin, Ontario NOB 1TO with the financial assistance of
The Canada Council and the Ontario Arts Council.

Distributed by The University of Toronto Press,
5201 Dufferin Street, Downsview, Ontario M3H 5T8.

Originally published as *Jargon 18* by Jonathan Williams,
Highlands, North Carolina, 1956.

Cover is after a photograph of Irving Layton by Sam Tata.

Printed and bound by The Porcupine's Quill.
The stock is Zephyr laid, and the type, Ehrhardt.

WHAT ELSE are you going to say about a man whose work you whole-heartedly admire than that he is a good poet? If you consider yourself a critic of poetry, which I do, all the more reason for speaking with all the force you can command in his support. You would be a fool to do less. When I first clapped eyes on the poems of Irving Layton, two years ago, I let out a yell of joy. He was bawdy but that wasn't why I gave him my recognition. But for the way he greeted the world he was celebrating, head up, eyes propped wide, his gaze roving round a wide perimeter – which merely happened to see some sights that had never been disclosed to me so nakedly or so well.

In writing of a good new poet for the first time the words come crowding to my mind, jostling together in their eagerness to be put down: He inhabits the medium and is at home in it, passionately; luxurious freedom, as of a huge creature immersed in an ocean that he knows he will never plumb and need never fear to reach the bottom of. This is poetry in which he lives unchecked. And he has eyes and he has power to penetrate wherever its lust leads him to satisfy its hungers. More moral men will fly off from a dish which is his natural food and which he takes with a laugh. May he never grow too delicate to take his fill of it and speak of his joy in it with a full appetite. That he is a man, and therefore must be guarded, he knows also. He laughs from a full belly. Not to be confined by a metaphor – he has been to the university and sat grinning and with moist eyes among his peers. He knows the Puritans and what they do and have done. He knows at least two religious beliefs, and how to practice all ten of them. In fact he knows the colours of the spectrum, and how all the colours are split off from it. If you want him to be true to yellow, he will be true to red; and if green, he will be true to purple or brown or black or the most heavenly blue. He has an unrivaled choice of words; an unusual vocabulary and the ability to use it. As far as deftness in the craft of a poet, I think he can do anything he wants to – except confuse himself with the mere sound of his own mouthings or delicate mincings or weighty sounding apostrophes. He is modest in facing the opinions of others – an enormous and increasingly rare virtue. He even respects Ezra Pound but has no inclination to imitate him. He despises Canada (being a Canadian), and loves and would give his heart for it. He loves women and speaks of it freely. They enjoy him also and double-cross and abandon him – and all this his poems show and speak of in the most meticulous English. He uses as much slang as suits his fancy or his need, and no more. He is not bound by the twentieth century if he does not find its language fitting to his purpose, and defies anyone who would bind him to that use. His structure of the poetic phrase is eclectic; that is to say, he does what he pleases with it, and there he possibly goes wrong. But what difference does it make, if he writes well? He has a quick and dogged wit which does not shun to soil its hands; in other words, he can be downright dirty if the occasion calls for it – as it frequently does in dealing with the nicer present-day wits of the United States. The metaphysicians, men and women who want to abandon a British or American way of talking, he is indifferent to – but the same is common with all present-day poets if they are worthy of the name.

Irving Layton has written profusely, pouring out his verses without check. That is the way to write, correcting one's self in the act of writing, the words, held as it were, in solution, latent, eternally in process of being formed. No constipation here – though the action of writing can be repeated and repeated and repeated in multiple draughts until, by sheer repetition, it finally becomes fluid. But that doesn't appear to be his way.

In short, I believe this poet to be capable, to be capable of anything. He's a backwoodsman with a tremendous power to do anything he wants to with verse. I have seen modern verse written in French and in the local dialects of the United States before which he must stand in awe. Lucky for such writers that he exists, for he will not be idle, but attack with his unsated egotism until he has subdued their challenges. There will, if I am not mistaken, be a battle: Layton against the rest of the world. With his vigour and abilities who shall not say that Canada will not have produced one of the west's most famous poets?

Can't say that it is my practice to read or to quote Blake, but I agree with him and with Layton, *'Praise is the practice of art.'*

William Carlos Williams, 1956

For Elizabeth, with Love

And me happiest when I compose poems.
Love, power, the huzza of battle
    are something, are much;
yet a poem includes them like a pool
    water and reflection.
In me, nature's divided things –
    tree, mould on tree –
    have their fruition;
I am their core. Let them swap,
bandy, like a flame swerve
I am their mouth; as a mouth I serve.

And I observe how the sensual moths
    big with odour and sunshine
    dart into the perilous shrubbery;
or drop their visiting shadows
    upon the garden I one year made
of flowering stone to be a footstool
    for the perfect gods
    who, friends to the ascending orders,
will sustain this passionate meditation
and call down pardons
for the insurgent blood.

A quiet madman, never far from tears,
    I lie like a slain thing
    under the green air the trees
inhabit, or rest upon a chair
    towards which the inflammable air
tumbles on many robins' wings;
    noting how seasonably
    leaf and blossom uncurl
and living things arrange their death,
while someone from afar off
blows birthday candles for the world

Filling their ears
With the immortal claptrap of poetry,
These singular lies with the power
    to get themselves believed,
The permanent bloom on all time-infected things;
Indicating the will to falsehood in the hearts of men,
The music in a pismire's walk, the necessary glory of dung,
    immortal coal of the universe,
Leibniz's mirroring monads, daybeams of consciousness

I see their heads sway at the seven o'clock lecture;
I imagine they forget the hungers, the desperate fears
    in the hollow parts of their bodies,
The physiological smells, the sardine cans, the flitch of bacon,
The chicken bones gathered neatly
                to one side of the plate;
Life is horrifying, said Cezanne,
                        but this is not
    what he meant who picked flowers blooming
    in the slaughterhouse; he meant the slit throats,
The bear traps smeared with blood, the iron goads, the frightened
    servant-girl's Caesarian,
And this planet dancing about Apollo,
    the blood drying and shining in the sun,
Turning to Titians, beauty, the Arts ...

My heart is parted like the Red Sea.
It cracks!
And where the cleft is formed
The BARBARI carrying their chromium gods
    on their sunburnt arms and shoulders
Ride on my nightmares, a hot desert wind
    pushing them swiftly toward these faces
    washed clean of Death and Agony;

God! God! Shall I jiggle my gored haunches
to make these faces laugh?
Shall the blood rain down on these paper masks?
Flammonde, Light of the World, in this well-lit
fluorescent age you are a failure, lacking savvy;
Gregor Metamorphosis, fantastic bogeylouse,
you are without meaning to those who nightly
bed down on well-aired sheets;
In the fifth row someone pulls out a laundered emotion
and wipes his long, false nose.

At last the bell goes, Lear lamenting Cordelia, the wall's
piercing cry ...

You may grieve now, gentlemen.

All day the heavens have opened up
and it has rained rained rained
rained
with the maliciousness of a minor poet.

It's not my element; I cannot live with it.
Perhaps because my forbears were thrifty merchants
it dispirits me to know
so much excellent water
        is going to waste, is going under bridges
to serve an outworn metaphor, expending
so much effort to so little effect.

Snow I can take, if I have to:
if only because of the satisfaction I have
in supposing that snow
is what someone has done to rain,
his contempt for it published in a million white bulletins.

It has rained for three days and three nights
and the vegetation is lush and very green.
They say Ireland is like that, the green rolling hillsides
a brogue in your eye and a lilt in both ears.
But I have never wanted to go to Ireland
now that her great sons are dead
(real Irish giants – Shaw and Joyce and Yeats – not
mythical ones)
and each little green blade, a rosary around it,
saying a paternoster to the wind.

Ireland? More like Africa.
I'm afraid to peer under my armpits, I might find
    tropical ferns growing sideways; and my limbs
    have begun to feel thick and rubberish and tubular.
I have the feeling if I step on the floor
                                of my room,
water will splash out of my ankles
as from an old boot or water bag.
The rain makes numerous thunders in my head,
    but it could be the tom-toms
    announcing the white man's love for the blacks.

Help me, someone.

I imagine my body is the whole steaming
                                continent of Africa,
and millions of animals are squishing
through the torrential jungle rains inside me
but one lion in particular
    I see him, the fierce proud beast –
roars, and roars again:
roars roars roars roars

When Love ensnares my mind unbidden
    I am lost in the usual way
On a crowded street or avenue
Where I am lord of all the marquees,
And the traffic cop moving his lips
    Like a poet composing
Whistles a discovery of sparrows
About my head.

My mind, full of goats and pirates
    And simpler than a boy's,
I walk through a forest of white arms
That embrace me like window-shoppers;
Friends praise me like a Turkish delight
    Or a new kind of suspender
And children love me
Like a story.

Conscience more flat than cardboard
    Over the gap in a sole,
I avoid the fanatic whose subway
Collapsed in his brain;
There's a sinking, but the madonna
    Who clings to my hairlock
Is saved: on shore the damned ones
Applaud with the vigour of bees.

The sparrows' golden plummeting
  From fearful rooftop
Shows the flesh dying into sunshine.
Fled to the green suburbs, Death
Lies scared to death under a heap of bones.
  Beauty buds from mire
And I, a singer in season, observe
Death is a name for beauty not in use.

No one is more happy, none can do more tricks.
  The sun melts like butter
Over my sweetcorn thoughts;
And, at last, both famous and good
I'm a Doge, a dog
  At the end of a terrace
Where poems like angels like flakes of powder
Quaver above my prickling skin.

It's all in the manner

>How a bold fly circles the greenleafed
>stalk: or the dog yawns and stretches
>in the sun: or my neighbour,
>his wife, like quiet monks, kneel
>before the chickpeas
>to weed, clean, again and again,
>the earth sockets
>   and their blazing cotyledons

>And it's how
>I dance my shanks, here, in the fields, reply
>to a question, tell some one off, piss
>open-legged, wake
>the dead with a yawp, B—,
>make love (One hand
>tied behind my back

It's all in the manner of the done

>Manner redeemeth everything: redeemeth
>man, sets him up among,
>over, the other worms, puts
>a crown on him, yes, size of a mountain lake,
>dazzling   more dazzling!
>than a slice of sun

1 Since the writings of wise men
   Are my chief study
   I am not like you, Li Po,
   A close observer of the habits of birds.
   On the other hand I am curious about people.
   I find their inexplicable cruelties
   A matter for sorrow and reflection.
       Nonetheless my lovers say
   The birds chirping in their green coverlets
   Gossip about my merry heart
   And to please me further exclaim
   They make nests from my smiles.
   Why is it I have never once heard
   Such reports about you
   Who have studied the doings of birds all your life?

2 To eat, drink, fornicate
   And to rail at priests –
   Was it for this
   I was shaped nine months
   In my mother's womb?

3 When I was young I quarrelled with everyone. I put
   Away my wife because she was fat and would not diet.
   I took up soldiering since killing was agreeable
   And the pay was good. When the victorious general
   Disbanded his troops I found a soft berth
   As his Keeper of Stores where my arrogant manner
   Earned respect from the several factions. Age
   And repeated sickness have at last brought me here.
   I have learned humility and compassion.
   Yet tell me, my sorrowful patient friend,
   When I was acquiring such distinguished virtues
   What were the long graveworms doing? Procreating.

4 This man loves intrigue.
 I have known him to upset a plan
 Which he himself in great secrecy had set afoot.
 In that way he maintains a good opinion of himself
 And feels himself masterful.

5 Having seen a drunkard stagger home,
 And a philosopher pitched headlong onto the street
 Because he could not pay the rent,
 And a poet befouling himself in the ditch
 I have shut myself away
   From such disturbing occurrences.
 All the motions of living are equally absurd
 But one might as well have clean linen.

MONT ROLLAND

Pitiless towards men, I am filled with pity
For the impractical trees climbing the exhausted hillside;
Sparse, dull, with blue uneven spaces between them,
They're like the beard of an uncombed tolerant monk,
            Or a Tolstoyan disciple, circa 1890.

Below these, a straggler, a tree with such enormous boughs
It might have remembered Absalom, who dead,
Put by the aping of his father's majesty;
And one lone cedar, a sycophant, stunted,
            A buffoon with sick dreams.

While all around me, as for a favoured intruder,
There's an immense silence made for primeval birds
Or a thought to rise like a great cloud out of a crater,
A silence contained by valleys,
            Gardes Civiles in green capes.

Nevertheless the Lilliput train trivializes
The tolerant monk, the trees, and this whirlpool of silence,
Though it fling over its side like a capitalist's bequest
A memorial row
            Of blossoming cherry trees.

And the highway which seen from my window seems
A suture in the flesh of a venerable patrician,
In the distance falls like a lariat on the green necks
Of the untamed hills, that raise like wild horses
            Their dignified, astonished heads.

Like
a memory
torn
at the shoulders,
my darling
wears
the chemise
I gave her –
a wedding gift.

At night
I tap out
my poems
on her hip bone.

When
she can't
sleep
either
we write
the poem
together.

I pass out of the door into the garden.
From my favourite tree one limb's broken.
An insect, egotist, strums his soliloquy
At my ear. I walk out under the open sky.

Theoretical man, my eyes have marked
Mounds of earth piled high and dark.
Earth, shovelsful – think of it –
In which to be born and buried.

Brown pods, brown leaves that lie
Beside quickening things, a king of parody
On them and their increasing passion:
But that's a thought that's out-of-season

When everywhere beyond my hands I see
Green shoots, conferva near the railway;
And grasses, young ferns, that sprout into air
Wispy as a twelve-year-old's pudendal hair.

CHOKECHERRIES

The sun's gift –

but the leaves a sickly green;
the more exposed curling, showing
a bleached white, many with ragged
holes;
Caterpillars have been
here
sliding their slow destructive bodies
over them.

I think of them, the leaves, as hoplites
or as anything ingloriously
useful,
suffering, dying ...

But the chokecherries,
ah;
Still, the leaves' sacrifice
is acrid on the tongue.

Who is that in the tall grasses singing
By herself, near the water?
I can not see her
But can it be her
Than whom the grasses so tall
Are taller,
My daughter,
My lovely daughter?

Who is that in the tall grass running
Beside her, near the water?
She can not see there
Time that pursued her
In the deep grasses so fast
And faster
And caught her,
My foolish daughter.

What is the wind in the fair grasses saying
Like a verse, near the water?
Saviours that over
All things have power
Make Time himself grow kind
And kinder
That sought her,
My little daughter.

Who is that at the close of the summer
Near the deep lake? Who wrought her
Comely and slender?
Time but attends and befriends her
Than whom the grasses though tall
Are not taller,
My daughter,
My gentle daughter.

No noise of rowlocks, no ecstasy of hands,
No sound of crickets in the inextricable air:
But a Roman silence for a lone drummer's call.

Now noiseless as a transaction, a brown hare
Breaks from the cold fields, bounds ahead;
Now slowly slowly the season unwinters
On its spool of white thread.

Lonely and fleshed with hates, who here
Would be God's angry man, a thundering Paul
When December, a toga'd Cato, slow to anger,
At last speaks the word that condemns us all.

By that, by this, by sharp ecstasies perplexed,
illumined, a saint streaked with foibles,
    I wore at the heart a hairshirt of fire,
wrapped my thighs in a loincloth of bees.

Honour foreswore and talent, and with these
burnished those bluedyed baubles which hang
    amorously from sad and arid bantam trees
in one-room apartments cheaply furnished.

Yet now with lust and indignation spent
and even remorse and other troubles
    I ask whether by deliberate will I went
or frenzy at a woman's beauty.

And cannot answer. But recall
a flaxen-haired boy five years old
    who one bad night put fire to his gown
and watched the flames about him rise blue and gold.

The solid hunchback, the poet said
(boarding the summer at Les Solitudes)
throws a bigger shadow on the ground
than any of us; moreover
the children enclose it like a corolla.

My dog licks his fur,
paws his torn ear

And the driftwood I perceive
in the spray and lifting mist, twisting tongues
licking the shore, only momently
blackens an antique lamp; rots
and settles back into the Heraclitean fire.

My dog licks his fur,
paws his torn ear

Fishermen, the original village
on their brows, small and dark with the hour,
row towards the urgent sun. There
all human cares dissolved they burn
like sheet metal in the burning lake

My dog licks his fur,
paws his torn ear

My glands that sweat pity, sweat
for oars greying in the sun, for old men
and clouds and in the cloud-filled lake
the ripple that breaks from its round sleep
like a child crying out from weariness.

My dog licks his fur,
paws his torn ear

Hourly such images flood the mind;
touch memory, detritus of appetite,
into fire; though destiny who plays it safe
uses always and only the same rigged wheel,
I gain incongruous poems and bells for buoys.

My dog licks his bruised fur,
paws his torn ear

VEXATA QUAESTIO

I fixing my eyes upon a tree
Maccabean among the dwarfed
    Stalks of summer
Listened for ships' sound and birdsong
And felt the bites of insects
    Expiring in my arms' hairs.

And there among the green prayerful birds
Among the corn I heard
    The chaffering blades:
'You are no flydung on cherry blossoms,
Among two-legged lice
    You have the gift of praise.

Give your stripped body to the sun
Your sex to any skilled
    And pretty damsel;
From the bonfire
Of your guilts make
    A blazing Greek sun.'

Then the wind which all day
Had run regattas through the fields
    Grew chill, became
A tree-dismantling wind;

The sun went down
    And called my brown skin in.

Wanting for their young limbs praise,
Their thighs, hips, and saintly breasts,
    They grow from awkwardness to delight,
Their mouths made perfect with the air
    About them and the sweet rage in the blood,
    The delicate trouble in their veins.

Intolerant as happiness, suddenly
They'll dart like bewildered birds;
    For there's no mercy in that bugler Time
That excites against their virginity
    The massed infantry of days, nor in the tendrils
    Greening on their enchanted battlements.

Golda, Fruma, Dinnie, Elinor,
My saintly wantons, passionate nuns;
    O light-footed daughters, your unopened
Brittle beauty troubles an aging man
    Who hobbles after you a little way
    Fierce and ridiculous.

There are brightest apples on those trees
    but until I, fabulist, have spoken
they do not know their significance
or what other legends are hung like garlands
    on their black boughs twisting
like a rumour. The wind's noise is empty.

Nor are the winged insects better off
    though they wear my crafty eyes
wherever they alight. Stay here, my love;
you will see how delicately they deposit
    me on the leaves of elms
or fold me in the orient dust of summer.

And if in August joiners and bricklayers
    are thick as flies around us
building expensive bungalows for those
who do not need them, unless they release
    me roaring from their moth-proofed cupboards
their buyers will have no joy, no ease.

I could extend their rooms for them without cost
    and give them crazy sundials
to tell the time with, but I have noticed
how my irregular footprint horrifies them
    evenings and Sunday afternoons:
they spray for hours to erase its shadow.

How to dominate reality? Love is one way;
    imagination another. Sit here
beside me, sweet; take my hard hand in yours.
We'll mark the butterflies disappearing over the hedge
    with tiny wristwatches on their wings:
our fingers touching the earth, like two Buddhas.

BACCHANAL

You there, and you, and you
Come, I want to embrace you
With beer on your breath and halitosis
Come with your Venus-rotted noses

Here is man's true temple, cool
Gloom, sincere worshippers –
Before them the tapers of beer
Like lights lit on many altars

Come, pleasure's my god and yours
Too, to go by your charming noises
Let's hiccup our happiness
And belch our ecstasies to Bacchus

He hears us and sends the room
Spinning. May his touch be always upon us.
May we, as he spins us in the cool gloom,
Be forever in his keeping.

Your eyes, heavy-lidded,
half-closed, make of sadness
itself a caprice, or seem to.
I have the feeling, miss,
you dream too much
of flight – on winter evenings!
Yet the mist
of those nerveless evenings
lives in your clouded eyes.

Your face
tilts toward the gay edifice
through whose casements
birds might go in and out;
and your elbow is,
to be sure,
a gesture that makes known
your will – yet hardly more;
the flexures of your breast and skirt
turn like an appetite also there.

Too small
for a swan, a raping Zeus:
the still bird, symbol
of decession and freedom,
that you fold between your full
breasts
pins you by a paradox
against the air.
There is no happiness here;

Only the desire
of the impotent, the weak
who, if they wish to speak,
must first grow indignant;
It taxes my brain,
miss, to guess at the monster
or tyrant
who inhabits the shuttered building
the lines of your head and breasts
turn away from with such disdain.

Unlike others, near cousins to fatuity,
you walked carelessly into my thoughts of you;
and with a tired movement of your eyelids
defined yourself to me
under your absurd hair.

To begin with, I had never seen
so much sadness on a woman's mouth.
There were no answers for your grief.
My curiosity like a trained domestic
left everything as before, as if untouched.

Though an incredible wound in the air
the bowl of apples on the garden table
sustained itself with simply being.
It is the architecture of sanity, I thought.
But you wove the air with charred fingers.

'The centrality of the fly,' you said,
'It's impassive, a black demi-god. The
flowers choke the weeds. No matter.'
The look on your face appalled at being there
has taught me severity, exactness of speech.

For saying this
curse me to see seven Canadian winters
  but your emptied stare
is the death of all poets. You, depthless,
and your face a school, a discipline,
  magic away the martyrdoms, dissipate
the tragic pneumas in my brain-box
to as little meaning as
    disturbed flox on wet sand.

Or hex me to see
the great black-bearded Agamemnon
  slain by a danceband leader
:bonged on the head on the polished floor:
yet wreathing your brittle fingers you make
  a sweatless funnel through which fall,
insubstantial, love, and mysterious
as the contempt for the harmless
    the desire to strike and dishonour.

Certainly, what fazes me
  even more than the satisfaction
you take in your throat and white shoulders
is that all dark verse,
    Hebrew or Sophoclean,
in your cascading neighbourhood seems
aberrant, out-of-keeping,
a lout or playboy
      if you know what I mean
discussing the schizoid features
of the Absolute.

MILDRED

'Beneath this huge oak
Your passion, my dear, seems trivial
And your vexation
Not important, not important at all.'

This is what I might have said
In words like these. But there was
A shadow in her face
Annealed like porcelain or glass

That held my tongue:
Oaks have a way of concealing
By a sudden tumult of leaves
What it is they are feeling –

With humans it's otherwise.
The darkening of lip or eye
The painedged voice
Are treacheries.

So I bid Mildred speak.
But she was silent
That windless day
As the unstirring oak.

'You'll not always remember
His hands, his eyes: things pass.
See how the sun's white body
Now lies rotting; there, in the deep grass.'

Two spots glowed in her cheeks.
Then she smiled, derisively;
And because she had much to say
Said nothing, turning her face away.

When my carefree three-years daughter
Came rushing upon a moth;
Crying and stumbling, she drove it toward us.
The child was out of breath.

She chased it on – on – into the fields
With wild imploring cries,
Pursued by my brute laughter
And Mildred's still derisive eyes.

Aware, love, on waking
How the hours can bring
The effectuation of only
One paradigm of things

Or to put it all
As sages do, metaphysically,
And talk of the potential
Becoming actuality

I must beg mercy, love,
When you offer me your eyes
Your lips for kissing
That I so surlily refuse

For this loss, this sacrifice
Is my commemorating stone
To all that might be
Yet this day will not be done.

She came to us recommended
By the golden minutes and by nothing else;
Her skin glowed, sang with the compliments
Which these same minutes paid her.

Her hair burned like a yellow fire
To celebrate the strange beauty of her face;
Herself, she walked unconscious
Of the need she started in us to praise, admire

The elegance we found in us
Like a vein of rare silver when we saw her;
But all our thoughts were caught in the compass
Of her royal arms and we sank down

Into the dark where the blood sings after dark,
Into the light because it was the light,
Into the clear valley where her body was made,
Her beauty had lain, now resurrected

Raised by the minutes which start, slay,
Their ivory hafts fiery with sun-motes
Which, crying, we seized to make an immortal ring
For beauty which is its own excuse and never dies.

POEM

I would for your sake be gentle
Be, believe me, other than I am:
What, what madness is it that hurls me
Sundays against your Sunday calm?

True, there's enough gall in my ducts
To cover an area, and more:
But why you – free from evil, poor bird?
Why you – my heart and saviour?

I swear I'm damned to so hate and rage.
But your fair innocence is my guilt;
And the stream that you make clear
I must, to fog my image, fill with silt.

Bear with me, bear with me –
Your goodness, gift so little understood
Even by the angels I suppose
And by us here somewhat undervalued

Is what I hold to when madness comes.
It is the soft night against which I flare
Rocketwise, and when I fall
See my way back by my own embers.

THE SATYR

My Lovely, my impossible Love,
In a lane in Kishinev
Three hundred years ago
Silent in a quiet place
An old Greek with light green eyes
And wrinkled face
Sits and stares and sees nothing at all.

The years fall before him like a decayed wall.

And resurrected in the rooms
Of gambling houses
The violins scrape
And the Magyar women are beautiful
And the Magyar women have kissable napes
Perfumed and beautiful their blouses.

Quadrilles, mazurkas play everywhere
Play with a bold, intoxicating air
I could put on a caftan
A red fez, a turban
And sweep you into my arms
Across the roofs and churches of St. Catherine.

Ah, what bands! what crowds!

I tell you, my inviolate Love,
Till you and I embrace,
This Greek, trouserless and undignified,
Too old himself to sing or dance
His quiet gaze lost in the distance
Must like some ill-used god
Smoke his infernal pipe
And turn his green insensate eyes on us.

And you and I smoulder and burn.

And if I say my dog's vivid tongue
Clapped the frogs under their green fables,
Or the rock's coolness under my hand
Told me clearly which way the sun passed

And if I say in a clean forest
I heard myself proclaimed a traitor
By the excellent cones for I thought
Where the good go, green as an apple

And if like our French grocer, Mailloux,
I lay these things on your white table
With a hot involuntary look,
And add a word about the first gods

I take satisfaction from your smile
And the indication of your shoulder
Before the birds leave off their singing
And slowly the dark fills up my eyes

But when you stand at night before me
Like the genius of this place, naked,
All my ribs most unpaganlike ache
With foolstruck Adam in his first wonder.

Not of drowning. But of the female element
that swaddles my limbs thrashing.
    I roll, a careless animal,
    in the green ointment;
face down, my forehead bringing
intelligence into this featureless waste.

Confident as all hell, I am made one
with the waves' enterprise: they
    bend over my bleached body
    like submarine masseurs.
Then calm. The sun embroiders us –
a brilliant lotus on shantung.

Or she's an Asian goddess, the river;
who slides her fat cheeks over my elbows,
    her green buttocks. I feel
    her deep vibrations as if a seaplane
had plunged his ruinous shadow
like a sword through her coiling body.

I fall from her clasp, shuddering,
a senseless interloper, afraid;
    see I shall rise on the water
    drowned, and dismally rise;
remember the face of my child, Adrian on the hill
and all his hens that were laying like mad.

It has taken me long, Lygdamus,
    to learn that humans, barring
a few saints, are degenerate
    or senseless.

The senseless ones are never by design
    evil; but get in your way
like the ugly stumps of trees; order
    bad taste or out of boredom
start long wars
                where one's counted on
to dredge up manliness, fortitude, and valour
    for their stupefactions.

But wicked are the clever ones.
    Cultured and adept
they will seduce a friend's dear one
with praises of her husband on their lips.

As for the wife
    a little alcohol parts her thighs.
Do not blame her: her husband's name
on the seducer's lips
    makes her the eagerer to satisfy,
teaches her she lies with her very spouse.
And that way is best: no pricks of inwit,
    but the novelty's stab of pleasure is there.

Therefore give me only lovers.
   Come, my latest one, sloe-eyed,
your firm breasts whirling like astonished globes
   before my eyes cross-eyed with lust;
though my legs are bandy
               the heart's stout
and this provocative member smooth and unwrinkled.
Till the morning parts us, I'll lie beside you
   your nipple at my tired mouth
and one hand of mine
            on your black curling fleece.

No one told me
to beware your bracelets,
the winds I could expect
from your small breasts.
No one told me
the tumult of your hair.
When a lock touched me
I knew the sensations
of shattering glass.

Your kissings put
blue waters around me.
I would look at you
with bold Cretan mirth:
I would forget
I am a cringing semite,
a spaniel suffering
about your tight skirts.

I slabber for your rippling
hips, your white shoulders.
I am sick
with love of you. Girl, o girl,
let our washed limbs make
a perverse Star of David
and cones of flesh,
Cythera all night
at my silvered back.

LATRIA

Give me, Dark One, these
A woman's white knees
A woman's fine eyes
Her hot, lathered thighs

The nuptial embrace
The first look of love
A bird, sparrow or dove,
The unscheming face

Any bloom, a rose,
Creation's frenzy
The thrill of pity
– The rest is prose.

MAXIE

Son, braggart, and thrasher,
is the cock's querulous strut
in air, an aggression.

At sight of him as at the sound
of 'raw' my mind half-creates
tableaus, seas, immensities.

Mornings, I've seen his good looks
drop into the spider's mitre
pinned up between stem and stem.

All summer the months grovel
and bound at his heels like spaniels.
All seasons are occult toys to him,

a thing he takes out of the cupboard
certain there are no more
than two, at the most four.

I suppose, spouse, what I wanted
was to hold the enduring folds
of your dress. Now there's this.

This energetic skin-and-bones. You'll see,
he'll pummel the two of us to death,
laughing at our wrinkled amazement.

Yes, though his upthrust into air
is more certain
than delight or unreason,

and his active pellmell feet
scatter promises, elations
of breast and womb;

yet his growing up so neighbourly
to grass, us, and qualifying cobwebs
has given me a turn for sculptured stone.

THE ANTS

I watched them
wriggling out
              of the
electroluxed dirt,

jots of life
whirled out of a vacuum –
a Time Machine –
on dead plateaus
on craters,

iotas of energy
black specks of determination
– – irresistible!

they lifted
concealed lids
and tossed them aside

they opened
mystified doors
in the slopes of mountains

they poised themselves
on withered rocks
as if waiting
for Time to begin:

retrieving their intuitions
in the hard grains of sand
they adjusted
their tiny grey helmets

then took soundings
and came down
guardedly, lacking
their usual assurance;

shook the carpet lint
from their polished bodies
contemptuously
as if to hear better,
                skeltering now
like African warriors;

at the edge
of the newspaper
their polished bodies
                gleamed
like tiny limousines

– – magnetized filings,
they waited
for signals.

I have studied history, he said.
I expect nothing from man
Save hecatombs.
C'est son métier. And ferity.

No longer perhaps to his own kind
But to the sulphur-coloured butterfly
And young seals, white, without defence –
To whatever crawls, flies, swims.

It is life itself offends this queer beast
And fills him with mysterious unease;
Consequently only half-movements
Delight him – writhings, tortured spasms

Or whatever can stir his derision
By defect or ungainliness
Or, maimed, flutters from weakness like a bird:
Say, a noble falcon, with splintered wing.

It is as if, killing, he looked for answers
To his discontent among severed veins
And in the hot blood of the slain
Sought to inundate forever his self-horror

Or like a sodden idiot who plucks
A thrush from a willow, grief in her green hair,
Throttles it to uncover the root of its song.

Let the gods who made him, pity him.

In August, while butterflies
Engage twig and rock;
Love-sheaths bloom in convenient fissures
On a desiccated stalk;
The generation of Time brings
Rind, shell, delicate wings

And mourners. Amidst this
Summer's babble of small noises
They weep, or interject
Their resentful human voices;
At timely intervals
I am aware of funerals.

And these iambic stones
Honouring who-knows-what bones
Seem in the amber sunlight
Patient and confounded,
Like men enduring an epoch
Or one bemused by proofs of God.

TO A VERY OLD WOMAN

Old woman, your face is a halo of praise
That excludes nothing, not even Death;
  I have looked upon your waxy and virginal torso
  And I see you now as a frail candle
Whose flame, the initial sputter of ignition over,
Burns gently and with composure.

So the first taste of death was bitter.
Now you burn with a composed glow
  Listening, half-amused like a superior person,
  To your bridegroom which is the Darkness
While each hour of your lovely embrace
Descends in ecstatic beads of silence.

Old woman,
What does he say, your bridegroom?

That his child, Death, grows in my womb.

What else, old woman?

That only my white and virginal skin
Seals off the darkness from the death within.

Old woman, with face ageless like snow,
What will you do now?

Flame serenely
Till like a warmed candle
I curve over
The arm of my hurrying bridegroom and lover.

Is that all, old woman?

Yes ...
No. When Death and Darkness embrace
Over me
I shall have no face
I shall be utterly gone.
Use the blackened wick
For a headstone.

DEATH OF MOISHE LAZAROVITCH

My father's coffin pointed me to this:
O arrogant with new life his black beard
Fierce and stiff and partner to the dark wood
Sent me the way to what I most had feared

Became at the last a ring of bright light,
A well whose wall of mourning faces turned
My sighs to silence to a deep wound
Which stained the outstretched figure as it burned.

I swear it burned! If not, why the bright light
Like a tall post that had caught the sun's ray?
White the figure was and bright O so bright,
I have not seen its equal since that day.

I do not know how they lifted him up
Or held the vessel near their mourning silk,
But their going was like a roar of flames
And Matter sang in my ears like poured milk.

THE MADONNA OF THE MAGNIFICAT

I shall wander all night and not see
    as much happiness as this infant gives
to his plain sisters who are adoring him
and his mother cradling and covering
    him with her love.

She has borrowed the white moon from the sky
    to pillow his golden curls
and at her magical cry the dark roofs
the length of the street lie down
    like quiet animals.

The night will wear out and disappear
    like soiled water through the city's drains
but now it is full of noise and blessed neighbours
and all the tenement windows fly open
    like birds.

IN MEMORY OF FRED SMITH

Alive, he daily spun
Schemes for the active bone
And went about arranging
The unchanging.

He fluttered his kite
Like any hopeful trotskyite;
Knew (Machine Age sciolist)
Sex and politics

And sampled the flawed
Ridottos o' the world
Like the melancholy cakes
Consumed at wakes.

For unreason occupies
A man until he dies;
Then healed but dumb
He learns a new equilibrium.

But I was known to him
Who loved my single aim:
His term accomplished
By that much am I diminished.

OVERHEARD IN A BARBERSHOP

'Nature is blind,
and Man
a shaggy pitiless ape
without Justice,'
the razored
old gentleman said,
his acidulous breath
fogging the barber's
round mirror.

As he talked
I remarked
the naevi, black
and dark purple,
on his crumbling face:
Death's
little victory flags.

Tired of chewing
the flesh
of other animals;
Tired of subreption and conceit;
of the child's
bewildered conscience
fretting the sly man;
Tired of holding down
a job; of giving insults,
taking insults;
Of excited fornication,
failing heart valves,
septic kidneys ...

This frosty morning,
the coffin wood bursting
into brilliant flowers,
Is he glad
that after all the lecheries,
betrayals, subserviency,
After all the lusts,
false starts, evasions
he can begin
the unobstructed change
into clean grass
Done forever
with the insult
of birth,
the long adultery
with illusion?

A dull people,
but the rivers of this country
are wide and beautiful

A dull people
enamoured of childish games,
but food is easily come by
and plentiful

Some with a priest's voice
in their cage of ribs: but
on high mountain-tops and in thunderstorms
the chirping is not heard

Deferring to beadle and censor;
not ashamed for this,
but given over to horseplay,
the making of money

A dull people, without charm or
ideas,
settling into the clean empty look
of a Mountie or dairy farmer
as into a legacy

One can ignore them
(the silences, the vast distances help)
and suppose them at the bottom
of one of the meaner lakes,
their bones not even picked for souvenirs.

Their dufflebags sprawl like a murder
Between the seats: themselves are bored
Or boisterous. These are ignorant soldiers
Believing that when forever the violent die
The good receive their inexhaustible cow –
Grade seven and superman have arranged everything.
The other passengers are unimportant liars:
Salesmen, admen, the commercial trivia,
Blown between the lines of memoranda,
And across the aisle, disposed on thirty beds,
Two limp virgins eyes below the navel.

Slowly the train curves around rich
Suburban Westmount that squats upon a slum,
Then like a hypodermic plunges past
Uniform fenceposts into open country;
There's glazed sunlight upon the hard serrated
Fields. Air is thin slightly neurasthenic
Over the distant indiscriminate trees
That posture on hillsides gross and secretive
As women staling. Pins withdrawn suddenly
Barns collapse like real estate models. The senses
Run like swift hares along the fences.

These are the fire-lands and this a sealed train
Of cold excursionists, throats buttoned up
With yellow timetables.
                                        On folded hands
The minutes drop like dandruff. The
Jetted column survives in a black foetus,
And the goats leap into their faces shrieking.

COMPLIMENTS OF THE SEASON

Returning with an annual passion
April winds suck buds, blow
Greenness into the palmate leaf and find
A passionate lady at dresser moulting.
Hair and cuticle stream with the season
Through her mirror.

Under the foraging sunlight
Humans rancid beside sweet-smelling trees
Sprawl between the thorns while Mount Royal
Slopes its green arms under their arses;
And the one-armed beggar
Brutal with red and yellow pencils
Dies with a windmill in his arms –
There were no shebas, not even jills.

At the base hospital behind the lines
Ideologies are carried out in bedpans;
And next april and the april after
The veterans of the two last wars
Will lay their crutches against the cross
That shines steadfast upon the city
With the faith of its shareholders.

Against the curbstones like thick nostrils
The sunlight begins to dry
This snotflecked world.

There were of course those whom ease
 or a default of imagination
had made optimistic:
the backbone of the country
but slightly bent with perplexity.

There was the Muse's stepchild,
 an amuser:
a price on his English beard,
on his viewable grimace.

Also the hack fabulist
with no gift of words
for us: gain
    his criterion.

And one, a one-lunged
trumpeter
   who denied
long, long before cockcrow
– hollow-chested.

And Cowardice hiding out
 behind a circus show of reason:
hardest he was to smoke out.

THE RED AND THE BLACK

When I slumped down on the cut grass
in the rich man's fancy golf course
I must have deranged a detail
of slumbering noonday mosquitoes
for they came at me with the distemper
                                    of outraged innocence;
storming my brown wrists and ankles
exposed like a Mexican bandit's
surrendering to the forces of law & order
– you've seen them, barefooted,
hands outstretched, holding their useless carbines.

Since they were stupid and greedy
it was no great matter to kill them;
but not before they had devised
thick welts that rose red on the soft flesh;
though in the outcry I thought
how like three shapely nuns
sharing a ball or a secret between them
the silky devouring ravens
                                    in the distance
walked away from the young poplar
– an arrow lodged in the bright turf,
its green feathers still quivering.

How shall I sing the accomplished waters
Whose teeming cells make green my hopes
How shall the Sun at daybreak marry us
Twirling these waters like a hoop.

Gift of the waters that sing
Their eternal passion for the sky,
Your exact beauty in a wave of tumult
Drops an Eden about your thighs.

Green is the singing singing water
And green is every joyous leaf
White myrtle's in your hand and in the other
The hairy apple bringing life.

ORIGINAL SIN

Because he was not made
into a detergent or blue lampshade
proud, proud
he represses a faint smile
– his wreath for those who died.

And because
he watched the vile impalement
of his father, this one
a veined light has in his eyes,
interesting to himself and others.

In the trembling brake
such an odd smile
have serpents in profile;
such a veined light
have their knitted coats.

Very merciful was the cancer
Which first blinding you altogether
Afterwards stopped up your hearing;
At the end when Death was nearing,
Black-gloved, to gather you in
You did not demur, or fear
One you could not see or hear.

I taught you Shakespeare's tongue, not knowing
The time and manner of your going;
Certainly if with ghosts to dwell,
German would have served as well.
Voyaging lady, I wish for you
An Englishwoman to talk to,
An unruffled listener,
And green words to say to her.

The afternoon foreclosing, see
The swimmer plunges from his raft,
Opening the spray corollas by his act of war –
The snake heads strike
Quickly and are silent.

Emerging see how for a moment
A brown weed with marvellous bulbs,
He lies imminent upon the water
While light and sound come with a sharp passion
From the gonad sea around the Poles
And break in bright cockle-shells about his ears.

He dives, floats, goes under like a thief
Where his blood sings to the tiger shadows
In the scentless greenery that leads him home,
A male salmon down fretted stairways
Through underwater slums ...

Stunned by the memory of lost gills
He frames gestures of self-absorption
Upon the skull-like beach;
Observes with instigated eyes
The sun that empties itself upon the water,
And the last wave romping in
To throw its boyhood on the marble sand.

Move, mademoiselle, with the wind,
move with the rivers: under
the clean sun the two keep fresh forever
and you pitching like a gull's wide wing
rise white and fathomless. Do not sit, pray,
   ever, as you do now, rigid, head
shoved forward and hands to one side
in a clasp of prayer: so, they
cannot unclose to feel the sudden gusts of wind
   or glide their eight good arches
of bone and blood for the rushing tides.

Here like two lilies in a day grown
dry, which yet not wholly dead no
Cyprian will shy at a trash heap
but keeps in a useless place your arms,
weightless, lean on the foetid air.
   Aloof, the begging hands stir
each other to a bliss the face being sad
declines, the lips opening
for a sigh, an O! as remarkable
   as the simple food
they say the ghost of Jesus had.

Sick defiant heathen and faithless, the
Faith put by for chaos whose sequel
is not a dancing star but green toxins;
the antinomies for a moment balanced
and all excesses cancelled out
   you sit queerly stable, intent
on the inner brawl and the single
familiar peal that holds you sane
as it comes reprieving each time creaking round;
   as one knocked silly by a blow
may fool the assaulter by looking quite serene.

The one is reticent, carries himself well;
Is free in manner, yet unapproachable;
    He makes us think certain temperate days
Can put a chill between the shoulderblades.
He uses courtesy like a knife.

Listen: for all his careful fuss,
Will this cold one ever deceive us?
    Self-hating, he rivets a glittering wall;
Impairs it by a single pebble
And loves himself for that concession.

The other, seemingly his opposite, grabs friend
Or cousin with an elastic hand;
    Is, if anything, ridiculous
In his intemperance to please:
Yet is to sovereign eyes his brother's brother.

For by unloading favours on
Friend and unsuspecting cousin
    He subverts each with guilt and crawls
Happily at last among equals.
He loves himself for the moist confession.

The cold one coming slowly down;
His brother, on knees, the easier to climb,
    Meet upon a safe and velvet stair:
All footfalls deadened, here's
No father's tread, and no terror.

Before me on the dancestand
A god's vomit or damned by his decrees
The excited twitching couples shook and
Wriggled like giant parentheses.

A pallid Canadienne
Raised a finger and wetted her lip,
and echoing the nickelodeon
'Chip,' she breathed drowsily, 'Chip, chip.'

Aroused, her slavish partner
Smiled, showed his dentures through sodapop gas,
And 'chip' he said right back to her
And 'chip, chip' she said and shook her ass.

Denture to denture, 'Pas mal'
They whispered and were glad, jerked to and fro:
Their distorted bodies like bits of steel
Controlled by that throbbing dynamo.

They stomped, flung out their arms, groaned;
And in a flash I saw the cosmos end
And last of all the black night cover this:
'Chip, chip' and a shake of the ass.

Five girls around a table.
One of them exhibits her fine teeth
Over a story. The Elohim made her.
Prepared this space and time for her.

And has the Elohim made a him for her?
Doubtless. The four others laugh.
Grow suddenly taut when they lift
Their cups mouthward: then spit out

Gobs of laughter as if the rims
Like fishhooks on a string
Had ripped the ha ha ohs
From their constricted throats.

GOLFERS

Like Sieur Montaigne's distinction
between virtue and innocence
what gets you is their unbewilderment

They come into the picture suddenly
like unfinished houses, gapes and planed wood,
dominating a landscape

And you see at a glance
among sportsmen they are the metaphysicians,
intent, untalkative, pursuing Unity

(What finally gets you is their chastity)

And that no theory of pessimism is complete
which altogether ignores them

Her face and teeth yellow from the christs
she embraces idiotically in her sleep;
her arms long and thin like wax tapers;
her eyes red, their sockets preternaturally deep.

Her lips cracked, from churning prayers;
the spittle – like pus in an infection –
manifesting how the soul has agents
to surround and grapple with each heavy sin.

On her untidy dresser pills by the dozen;
medicaments, loose hairs, syrups 'pour la rhume';
encompassing me, a sour body odour
vindicating empirical Hume.

Poor ignorant lass whom evil priests
like incubi from a foetid ditch
have sucked dry and left your very nipples
mis-shaped, and black as the hat of a witch.

ON SEEING THE STATUETTES OF EZEKIEL
AND JEREMIAH IN THE CHURCH OF NOTRE DAME

They have given you French names
   and made you captive, my rugged
troublesome compatriots;
   your splendid beards, here, are epicene,
plaster white
      and your angers
unclothed with Palestinian hills quite lost
in this immense and ugly edifice.

You are bored – I see it – sultry prophets
   with priests and nuns
(What coarse jokes must pass between you!)
   and with those morbidly religious
i.e. my prize brother-in-law
              ex-Lawrencian
pawing his rosary, and his wife
sick with many guilts.

Believe me I would gladly take you
   from this spidery church
its bad melodrama, its musty smell of candle
   and set you both free again
in no make-believe world
         of sin and penitence
but the sunlit square opposite
alive at noon with arrogant men.

Yet cheer up Ezekiel and you Jeremiah
    who were once cast into a pit;
I shall not leave you here incensed, uneasy
    among alien Catholic saints
but shall bring you from time to time
                        my hot Hebrew heart
as passionate as your own, and stand
with you here awhile in aching confraternity.

SUMMER IDYLL

At home, lying on my back,
Lying with perfect stillness I saw
The scene dispose itself differently
Like a backdrop held by an enormous claw:
On either side the even expensive
Sod; the bungalow with the red border
Of roses; the woman past her middle years
In gaberdine shorts, and her hard fists
That held in place over her suntanned knee
A book, half-shut, in spectacular covers.

And building up the summer afternoon
Music that came thudding upon the air
Music that came it seemed from nowhere
But came in fact from the vacant bedroom
And came from a persistent gramophone tune

Did I contrive this, or did I inerrantly see
The line of hair on her lip?
Surmise her frown? Her talipes?
Did the enchanted hour suddenly darken?
And did the roses
Really uncurl and stretch upon their stems
And order their ignorant centres
Toward the chill anonymous tune,
Then abruptly with the afternoon
Erupt into thick ash against the window frames?

Where's the poem, my companion said,
Which yesternight made me cry out
Like a sick bride or child, naked
Before you and that moneyed lout
Who smiled into his broad palm to see
A man might be touched by poetry.

And at that, two sick ravens flew
From my companion's eyes, curtsied
As only ravens can, then grew
Small, smaller than a pepper seed;
Crooked fowls that have flown from hell
I saw their trace on his black lapel

And knew that he'd lived with his shame
A day. Man, I cried, here's the poem
Which if now read without the flame
You will curse for a shapeless stone;
From mixed emotions I made that song,
Like yourself weak where I would be strong.

But my companion laughed out loud:
I am disgraced in my own eyes
To have dropped tears worth a cloud
For versicle as weak as this,
And brushed the pepperplumes angrily.
Nor has he spoken to me from that day.

In want of an author's omniscience
They strove with shadows in the fast-dying light;
But the shadows were themselves, things of time,
Which they cast without courtesy at each other's feet.

I saw them in the rain, near other debris,
The rusted cans the drops ping'd accurately and often;
There behind the house outlasting architects
The weather and the angry voices flayed them.

Now the children were spies to be outsmarted;
Neighbours grew suddenly in the air
Or in the trees, where the scrupulous robins
Kept signalling to them that they were there.

The leaves twitched to the words like wolves' ears
And gulped them down in heavy swallows,
Till they were open to every passer-by
And naked and humble as the grass.

Then they were quiet: quarrelling dogs,
I thought, silenced at the approach of men;
After a moment to catch furious breath
They will go at it hound-and-bitch again.

But I was wrong. In the end seeing
That they were finite as the rusting canisters
They solved the monstrous riddle of time and self
And forgave the hour and the changed weather.

For the point of view, they saw, was everything,
Though necessarily final. Yet the good life holds:
Like great art, is unsensational; and there time
Does not rush upon us but unfolds.

Below this broad street inverted bell-jars
Hanging from wooden crucifixes drop
Tiny moons upon the shaven asphalt;
Rouged whores lean lips to narrow slits: they stop
The young soldier with his bag of salt.

Under the night's carapace, the soft lanes
Are listening ears where sudden footfall
Starts a choir of echoes. A red light winks
Viciously; and the wind's occasional
Sigh lifts from the garbage pails their stinks.

Here private lust is public gain and shame;
Here the Oriental and the skipjack go;
Where those bleak outposts of the virtuous
The corner mission and the walled church grow
Like hemorrhoids on the city's anus.

O reptilian street whose scaly limbs
Are crooked stairways and the grocery store,
Isolate, is your dreaming half-shut eye:
Each virgin at the barricaded door
Feels your tongue-kiss like a butterfly.

Neither tribal nor trivial he shouts
From the city's center where tramcars move
Like stained bacilli across the eyeballs,
Where people spore in composite buildings
From their protective gelatine of doubts,
Old ills, and incapacity to love
While he, a Joshua before their walls,
Sells newspapers to the gods and geldings.

Intrusive as a collision, he is
The Zeitgeist's too public interpreter,
A voice multiplex and democratic,
The people's voice or the monopolists';
Who with last-edition omniscience
Plays Clotho to each gaping customer
With halcyon colt, sex crime in an attic,
The story of a twice-jailed bigamist.

For him the mitred cardinals sweat in
Conclaves domed; the spy is shot. Empiric;
And obstreperous confidant of kings,
Rude despiser of the anonymous,
Danubes of blood wash up his bulletins
While he domesticates disaster like
A wheat in pampas of prescriptive things
With cries animal and ambiguous.

His dialectics will assault the brain,
Contrive men to voyages or murder,
Dip the periscope of their public lives
To the green levels of acidic caves;
Fever their health, or heal them with ruin,
Or with lies dangerous as a letter;
Finally enfold the season's cloves,
Cover a somnolent face on Sundays.

When it came to Santayana's turn he,
His stomach cancer-riddled, turning sod
Upon the Sisters' white linen, canvassed God,
The Essences and Immortality,

Unriddling to the last. Brave philosopher,
As you piped your wisdom to friends your breath
Doubtless was heavy with puke, taint of death.
But I mean you no discourtesy, Sir.

Socrates did no better with a jest
About a cock; though artful Plato
And seminars've made that damn bird crow
For every longhead pegging out. My guest,

The world's, fare well in Limbo. You dead,
I shall want that bright eye, that huge bald head.

I read some famous Montenegrin duke
has intuitions about a peace. Hurrah.
But when May comes I close my eyes to walk
   over the bodies of lovers
   slim and languorous
whose naked skins soft to the soles of my feet
make the toes curl in at the rose nipples.

The waitress who genuflects like a nun
rubs the dado clean from customers' grease
till the wood glows with her own devotion;
   and a scent imprisoned
   between her breasts
leaps over the wall of her collar
to flee along the galleries of my nose.

Behind her back gleam the Silex cups:
helmets of that defunct Wilhelm;
and on the firm aluminum prop
   the coffee orbs,
   the liquid pouring in,
slowly acquire a religious look
black and reproving as her own.

LOVE'S DIFFIDENCE

Love is so diffident a thing.
I scoop up my hands with air;
I do not find it there
Nor in my friend's pleasure
Nor when the birds sing.

I am confused, forsaken.
I have lost the way.
Love's not as some men say
In woman's eyes, blue or gray;
Nor in kisses given and taken.

Love, I call out, find me
Spinning round in error.
Display your dank, coarse hair,
Your bubs and bulbous shoulder.
Then strike, witless bitch, blind me.

Vain and not to trust
unstable as wind,
as the wind ignorant;
shallow, her laugh
jarring my mended teeth.
I spit out
the loose silver
from my aching mouth.

With candid gaze
she meets my jealous
look, and is false.
Yet I am lost, lost.
Beauty and pleasure,
fatal gifts,
she brings in her thighs,
in her small amorous body.

O not remembering
her derision of me,
I plunge like a corkscrew
into her softness,
her small wicked body
and there, beyond reproach,
I roar like a sick lion
between her breasts.

'I'm the sort of girl
   you must first tell you love.'
'I love you,' I said.
She gave herself to me then
   and I enjoyed her on her perfumed bed.
By the gods, the pleasure in her small
     wriggling body was so great,
  I had spoken no lecherous falsehood.
Now not I nor my beloved,
    such is our heat,
can wait for either words or scented sheet
but on her or my raincoat go roughly to it.

I adore you, Marilyn.
You teach sex is no sin
Nor that anguishing fire
To which the saints aspire;
You make absurd for us
All love that's chivalrous:
There is more wisdom
In your shapely bum.
Real pleasure and goodness
Are in your rippling breasts,
Animal health and pride
In your magnificent stride.
Wench, you teach the race to know
Forms forbidden Plato,
A music of the stars
Locked from Pythagoras.

For those denying sex
Or lost in politics,
For the intellectual
Writing on the Fall
Or stilted volumes on
Sarah Hutchison;
For the sulky christian;
The arrogant, the fool
Disparaging his tool;
For the inhibited
Twisted by a simple need;
For all those who hate
Man's natural estate
Or lined with inner guilt
Trail, as some bugs do, filth:

O cinema goddess
More lovely than Venus,
More explosive than
Deirdre or Helen;
O beauteous wench, embrace
Me in an hour of grace,
Bounce me like the ocean
On each surprising limb;
Then let your kisses fall
Like summer rain on all;
Teach us the happiness,
The carnal blessedness,
The warmth, love, sanity
Of your redeeming energy:
Blest of women, earth goddess,
Teach us to delight and praise.

Your body to hold, your perfect breasts.
Your lips; your hips under my pregnant hands
    That when they move, why, they're snakes
Sliding, and hiding near your golden buttocks.

Then as your great engines of love begin
Intestinal, furious, submarine
    They spark into small bites
Whose hot spittle inundates all my deserts.

And I'm like water in a scoop of stone
Kissed into absence by a drying sun;
    Or I'm dried Sahara sand
Wanting your wetness over me without end.

So possessed, so broken's my entire self
No rosy whipcord, love, can bind my halves
    When queen you squat: you moisten
My parched nipples into a blazing garden.

And I your paramour-Paracelsus
Fish a soul for you from between my loins;
    You shudder in my embrace
And all your wetness takes the form of tears.

One night beside her spouse suddenly
Her heart was ambushed and her naked
Buttocks quivered with death's agony;
Her shoulders twitched she gave a low cry.
Love's frolic the weak churl thought and shed
Hot seed against her indifferent thigh.

The thing could barely stand. Yet taken
from his mother and the barn smells
he still impressed with his pride,
with the promise of sovereignty in the way
his head moved to take us in.
The fierce sunlight tugging the maize from the ground
licked at his shapely flanks.
He was too young for all that pride.
I thought of the deposed Richard ii.

'No money in bull calves,' Freeman had said.
The visiting clergyman rubbed the nostrils
now snuffing pathetically at the windless day.
'A pity,' he sighed.
My gaze slipped off his hat toward the empty sky
that circled over the black knot of men,
over us and the calf waiting for the first blow.

Struck,
the bull calf drew in his thin forelegs
as if gathering strength for a mad rush ...
tottered ... raised his darkening eyes to us,
and I saw we were at the far end
of his frightened look, growing smaller and smaller
till we were only the ponderous mallet
that flicked his bleeding ear
and pushed him over on his side, stiffly,
like a block of wood.

Below the hill's crest
the river snuffled on the improvised beach.
We dug a deep pit and threw the dead calf into it.
It made a wet sound, a sepulchral gurgle,
as the warm sides bulged and flattened.
Settled, the bull calf lay as if asleep,
one foreleg over the other,
bereft of pride and so beautiful now,
without movement, perfectly still in the cool pit,
I turned away and wept.

ENEMIES

The young carpenter
          who works on his house
has no definition for me.

I am for him
          a book. A face in a book.
Finally a face.

The sunlight
          on the white paper
The sunlight on the easy

Summer chair
          is the same sunlight
which glints rosily

From his hammer.
          He is aware suddenly
of connections: I

Am embroiled
          in the echoing sound
of his implement

As it slides nails
          into the resistant wood
from which later, later

Coffins will emerge
                as if by some monstrous
parturition. Is it any wonder

He so mislikes me
                seeing his handiwork
robed in black?

Seeing I shatter
                his artifact of space
with that which is

Forever dislodging
                the framework for
its own apprehension?

Over the wall
                of sound I see
his brutal grin of victory

Made incomplete
                by the white sunlit
paper I hold on my knee.

He has no metal
                gauge to take in
a man with a book

And yet his
        awkward shadow
falls on each page.

We are implicated,
        in each other's presence
by the sun, the third party

(Itself unimplicated)
        and only for a moment
reconciled to each other's

Necessary existence
        by the sight
of our neighbour's

Excited boy
        whom some God, I conjecture,
bounces for His joy.

GOD, WHEN YOU SPEAK

God, when you speak, out of your mouth
drop the great hungry cities
whose firetrucks menace my dreams;
where Love, abandoned woman, hatless and void,
snares me with her thousand pities;
ambulances pick up my limbs.

When you speak, you put phantoms
before me, unloyal friends who smile and envy;
great clouds crushed between my opulent arms
have not washed out deceit
or the barbed recollections of guilt, but
have wet me through for my ambition.

When you speak, I turn monument
to all my years misspent and good;
lovers have scratched their names
upon my base, birds have come and gone;
stationed at Place d'Armes or
the civic square I have sweat the same.

Curse all statues that rigid
Whether as flesh or angel's wings
stand their weight of stone upon the moment:
speak, yet now let all be unpinned again
to flow like colours from an exposed frame
into the earliest pools of morning.

Faces I too have seen in clouds
And on the walls of an outhouse;
And this morning I saw a frog
Deadstill, showing its moist, grey
Belly to some twigs and dry straw;
And a young terrified grass-snake
That threw off M's and bright S's
At the exact ferns as it streaked
Across my black boot into sedge.

To begin with there are the mysteries;
Though Klee recommends character
And Maritain has one lattice
That gives upon a monastery.
They write well: moreover, Klee paints.
To make a distinction, I think
Then that the poet transfigures
Reality, but the traffic cop
Transcribes it into his notebook.

In any case I'm adjusting
My organs to the future. Lies?
No: Language. The great days of Liz
Are mere Marlovian bombast:
The truth is dung, bubonic plagues
And London a stinking midden;
The maids unwashed and credulous,
The men coarse, or refined and corrupt
Reading their folios.

Sure I've come upon calyxes
And calicos, and melonrinds,
And fruitstones that reminded me
Of the bleeding heads of soldiers;
I've sworn then by the blood and balls
Of Christ and shouted eurekas
Till seven beavers watered me,
Putting out the fires. I've prayed,
Prayed and wept like a lunatic.

So I come back to the white clouds
And the outhouse wall. One may see
Faces anywhere if one's not proud.
The big words? I'd rather find lips
Shaping themselves in the rough wood;
Or connect my manshape's shadow
Floating like a fish under me
With – fish! Or think the day closes
Like the sad, red eyes of your English cocker.

SARATOGA BEACH

Knowing that the blade dies
Makes our kind unkind or wise
And writhe in the white fear
Of the death-knowing terror,
Of the flukes that tunnel in
The human imagination.

There is no escape from this.
Each out of his nothingness
Like bankrupt with creditor
Conspires with Death for power;
Ekes from the day's cruelty
His small immortality.

The insubstantial armies
The high wind today raises,
Grey manshapes of sand
Dissolving: this too's our end.
We hate, are insignificant.
But you, dear boys, are innocent.

Innocent as the flower-
Mauling bee of this hour,
As the self-indulgent waves
And the worm-eating sparrows;
And pleased as a naturalist
Whom randy lions have kissed.

For you this wind and water
Do not impugn all laughter.
They tell no tales. Clean of limb,
You play ball on the beach, swim,
Laugh at anything, are gay
At the sand column's disarray.

This, then, is my goodbye wish:
Calm not harsh through bitterness
Of gross finitude grow. Be
Fresh and changing as the sea.
Clear-eyed. Truthful. Go, children,
Improve your conversation.

BOYS BATHING

At a distance, dark;
each as the philosophers
would remind us
a compendium of history.

Not like the dead bass
I saw afloat,
its history
what my eye made for it.

One bounces like a porpoise,
the tallest ones
race for the boat:
squeals, unselfconsciousness.

But the youngest stops,
smiles at himself vaguely; at,
below the surface, the boulders
breathing like fish.

The sun is bleeding to death,
covering the lake
with its luxuriant blood:
the sun is dying on their shoulders.

Like Barbarossa's beard bright with oil
The maples glisten with the season's rain;
The day's porous, as October days are,
And objects have more space about them.

All field things seem weightless, abstract,
As if they'd taken one step back
To see themselves as they literally are
After the dementia of summer.

Now hale and sinewy my son, his friend
(The construction sand making a kind of
Festival under their feet) in their
Absorbed arm-on-shoulder stance

Look I think for all the world
Like some antique couple in a wood
Whom unexpected sibyls have made rich
(Something perhaps dressed up by Ovid)

On on condition, alas:
                    they'll not use
The gold but hold it as a memorial
To Chance and their own abstinence.

As our terrorized bodies sought the floor
And we lay prone near the pilasters
We saw the handsome chivalrous Nick
Who was that much younger and vainer

Than the rest of us
Rise up to confront the bearded outlaw;
A gun barked in the obscure element
And the bullet spurted towards him

Like a red spaniel maddened by pain,
And when we looked up we saw
Our brave and silly friend, Nicholas,
Execute a kind of piaffer

On the waxed belly of the dancefloor;
Only it was air he was holding
Languidly, distractedly in his arms
And when he fell we knew that he was dead.

THE DANCERS

Through envy
Of the propulsive movement
        Of your hips
You have swept
All other dancers
From the center
        Of the naked ballroom;
The glass-fluted table
In the feline shadows
        And the white leopards
Applaud you under the pagan chandeliers;
Moreover you have made
A pie-eyed poet weep
        From a loss of balance.

What more do you want or need,
My tuxedo'd Alpha,
My flaring red-dressed Omega,
Perfect, gifted with gracefulness,
Your genitals moist with dancing?

At the explosion of Peel & St. Catherine
O under the green neon signs I saw
        the ruined corpses of corpulent singers
arise from their tight mounds, sigh and
stumble upon each other dragging
their tattered shadows in their arms

They moved their bony mouths like the
fatalistic bulbs going on & off; teeth
        fell from their jaws, fell with such roars
it stirred the carpenters on the sleeping hills
who straightaway thought of the failure of nails
and the rubigo of all boards

What made the whiteflakes change
direction above my head? A flock
        of ravens shriek under the tramcar
and a lock turn in the air? Madness,
ah, a newsvendor, melting the snowflakes
came towards me & my distaste for winter

Or was it my spouse among the frenzied shoppers
looking at the white columns of lost & found
        for the eyes with which I first beheld her?
This night who ... what bankrupt
will sell her small diamonds to fill
my unresisting sockets when I am dead?

I draw near some woman shawled & shivering
and flakes of sorrow in her empty palms:
        'Ah, come home, come home, love,' I mutter.
'Here in my arms, mouth to mouth, we'll make
the splendidest tree that ever was
for this or any other Christmas.'

And raising my hand above the teeth
that rolled like cigarette butts in the wind
    I made, lo! the Cross which inflames our city
plunge hideously through the electric air
and turn into windowlights which glowed only
through the recollection of a former brightness

All night, all night the autos whizzed past me
into heaven, till I met men going there
    with golden nails and ravens whose wings
brushed the night up the tall sides of buildings
and behind them in the morninglight the windows shone
like saints pleased with the genius that had painted them.

THE COLD GREEN ELEMENT

At the end of the garden walk
the wind and its satellite wait for me;
their meaning I will not know
    until I go there,
but the black-hatted undertaker

who, passing, saw my heart beating in the grass,
is also going there. Hi, I tell him,
a great squall in the Pacific blew a dead poet
    out of the water,
who now hangs from the city's gates.

Crowds depart daily to see it, and return
with grimaces and incomprehension;
if its limbs twitched in the air
    they would sit at its feet
peeling their oranges.

And turning over I embrace like a lover
the trunk of a tree, one of those
for whom the lightning was too much
    and grew a brilliant
hunchback with a crown of leaves.

The ailments escaped from the labels
of medicine bottles are all fled to the wind;
I've seen myself lately in the eyes
    of old women,
spent streams mourning my manhood,

in whose old pupils the sun became
a bloodsmear on broad catalpa leaves
and hanging from ancient twigs,
    my murdered selves
sparked the air like the muted collisions

of fruit. A black dog howls down my blood,
a black dog with yellow eyes;
he too by someone's inadvertence
      saw the bloodsmear
on the broad catalpa leaves.

But the furies clear a path for me to the worm
who sang for an hour in the throat of a robin,
and misled by the cries of young boys
      I am again
a breathless swimmer in that cold green element.

Poets of a distant time
Mix madness with your rhyme
And with my dust I'll weave
    Dark rhymes for your reprieve

God was not Love nor Law,
God was the blood I saw,
The ever-flowing blood
    Staining water and sod

Woman I loved. Enough
She made me dream of love
And in that sexual dream
    Forget the whitethroat's scream

Saw men could finer sing
For someone's suffering
Laugh with you and after
    Envy you for your laughter

O these talented beasts
Might on your dead eyes feast,
Or pluck them from your head
    Plant jonquils in their stead

And with your dying spasm
Sing loose their gates of prison
Yet this transforming song
    Engender bitter wrong

Saw they could demolish
With love love's foliage
And that the poet's heart
   Has nowhere counterpart

Which can celebrate
Love equally with Death
Yet by its pulsing bring
   A music into everything

It was a neat trick
The glass of beer floating through the air
And coming to rest on my round table –
I spit on your one good eye Polyphemus –
Then the foam fell away from the rocks
To the sound of the drinkers' voices
Like the noise from the throats
Of a thousand flushed lavatories singing together
I could see their fishhook eyes menacing me
Sly at the bottom of the cool gloom of the tavern
But I wanted to write something on the waves
Carried towards the shore on the backs of a million snails
For I knew that arrived there
They would go begging like a long poem.

To the movement then of dark and light
A Byzantine angel slid down from the smoky wall
Hovering over me with his wings outstretched –
But I saw the shape where the flat tiles were not –
Before I could make a salt out of my astonishment
There was a meadow of surf in the bay of my elbow
And while the hungry robins picked at the air
White blossoms fell on their sad faces

Held in a frame of grass and ground for sentimental poets
Who weep when they are told of such things.

I do not remember when I first noticed
The human smell below the eyes
But the ghost of an unhappy sailor
That sometimes uses my body for a night's lodging
Blew a fistful of spray into the corridor
An eye started to twinkle like a crazy lighthouse
Rocked by a giant and the waves to bob
All around me like lopped heads
Their hair as they came to the surface combed down
Like Russian peasants tolled to a green Sunday church
I think someone called me brother
And pressed my hand clammy with many misfortunes
He must have seen the smoke curling
From my ears and from my mouth too
For he or someone who resembles him closely
Suddenly began to shout fire to the lavatories.

Heaven bless the three angels who lifted me up
Though my body turned into a picnic table
With six boyhood legs on St. Helen's Island
I heard their wings brushing the foam off the rocks
But they or the boys who had drowned that summer
Made too much noise
For the robins left off picking the air
And the blossoms decomposed at my feet into a bad odour.

As the afternoon wore on,
The wind rose like an American tariff;
I, more credulous than my parents,
Sat on my gardenstool, hoping for signs;
Something perhaps to fall out of the sky –
An eagle, like a piece of gunmetal,
Cracking the wall of air, flashing
The forbidden message from broken wings –
Perhaps a never-before-seen snake; or at the least,
A typewriter in the tall grass, its keys
Plucked by a legion of dry crickets;
But all I saw were great swathes of shadow
Moving across the fields like escaped jailbirds.

All afternoon
I watched the Mediterranean sky
Dotted with soft silver-ringed clouds
Like Greek city states,
Like white garlands for an Athenian holiday.
But look! In the north the Macedonian king
Has fastened his grey tunic
And moves slowly, slowly down the Thracian plains,
An armourer gathers the crimson daggerblades,
The heavens darken, and all about me
The rabblegrass, abject,
Whitens under the cruel skywind.

O helmeted goddess,
My little one, head nesting on arm,
I am afraid.

RECONCILIATION

Betwixt the harbour
and the great Crucifix
the snow falls
white and astringent.

I can not cancel
this wind
nor the wild cries
of the pitiful men
that fling themselves
against the Cross

hang there a moment
lighted Christs
and fall like tears
down the mountain's sides.

You are like my city
full of perverse appetites,
devout, beautiful:
cobras coiled in the snow,
white foxes, priests' surplices;

and in the tinfoil air
I doubly marvel
that after estrangement
should come
such fine unhoped-for
delirium.

In the midst of my fever, large
    as Europe's pain,
The birds hopping on the blackened wires
    were instantly electrocuted;
Bullfrogs were slaughtered in large numbers
    to the sound of their own innocent thrummings;
The beautiful whores of the king
    found lovers and disappeared;
The metaphysician sniffed the thought before him
    like a wrinkled fruit;
And the envoys meeting on the sunny quay
    for once said the truth about the weather.
In the midst of this rich confusion, a miracle happened: someone
    quietly performed a good deed;
And the grey imperial lions, growling, carried
    the news in their jaws.
I heard them. So did Androcles.

O from the height of my fever, the sweat
    ran down my hairless limbs
Like the blood from the condemned patron
    of specially unlucky slaves. Then, O then
Great Caesar's legions halted before my troubled ear,
    Jacobean in Time's double exposure.
My brassy limbs stiffened
    like a trumpet blast; surely
The minutes now covered with gold-dust
    will in time
Drop birdlime upon the handsomest
    standard-bearer,
Caesar himself discover the exhaustible flesh,
    my lips
White with prophecy aver before him.
But the conqueror's lips are like pearls,
    and he hurls his javelin at the target sky.

In the depth of my gay fever, I saw my limbs
    like Hebrew letters
Twisted with too much learning. I was
Seer, sensualist, or fake ambassador; the tyrant
    who never lied
And cried like an infant after he'd had to
    to succour his people.
Then I disengaging my arm to bless,
In an eyeblink became the benediction
    dropped from the Roman's fingers;
Nudes, nodes, nodules, became all one,
    existence seamless and I
Crawling solitary upon the globe of marble
    waited for the footfall which never came.
And I thought of Time's wretches and of some
    dear ones not yet dead
And of Coleridge taking laudanum.

Below me the city was in flames:
the firemen were the first to save
themselves. I saw steeples fall on their knees.

I saw an agent kick the charred bodies
from an orphanage to one side, marking
the site carefully for a future speculation.

Lovers stopped short of the final spasm
and went off angrily in opposite directions,
their elbows held by giant escorts of fire.

Then the dignitaries rode across the bridges
under an auricle of light which delighted them,
noting for later punishment those that went before.

And the rest of the populace, their mouths
distorted by an unusual gladness, bawled thanks
to this comely and ravaging ally, asking

Only for more light with which to see
their neighbour's destruction.

All this I saw through my improved binoculars.

THE IMPROVED BINOCULARS: History as the Long View.

What the Departing Crowds Might Have Seen ...

THE ORIGINAL EDITION of *The Improved Binoculars* appeared in 1956[1] under the imprint of Jonathan Williams, himself more poet and artistic personality than publisher, who operated on the strange and fluid peripheries of Black Mountain College in North Carolina. The book is identified as *Jargon 18* and is thus part of a series that included Charles Olson, Robert Creeley, Buckminster Fuller and Kenneth Patchen among its better-known contributors. The place of publication was Highlands, North Carolina, a location close to Black Mountain College, but also the site of the summer home of Williams' parents, and a place at which the peripatetic Williams[2] fetched up from time to time.

---

[1] There was to be a quick second edition with thirty additional poems which is identified on the inside front flap of its cover as a 'Second Printing', and which, while it bears 1956 as its publication date on the title page is described as a 'Second edition of 1000 copies' and is dated Winter 1957 on its last page. Contact Press is shown as the Canadian distributor, and Gael Turnbull's Migrant Books is listed as the agent in Britain.

[2] Jonathan Williams, poet, designer, photographer and literary traveller, began his artistic career as a student at the Institute of Design in Chicago in 1951. He drifted to Black Mountain College, which is best described as an experiment in creative education, where he fell under the spell (but not necessarily the influence) of the enormous presence of Charles Olson. In 1952, Williams was inducted into the US Army and was stationed in Stuttgart, Germany where, with the help of a small inheritance, he started the Jargon series of publications. After his discharge Williams drifted back to Highlands and Black Mountain College where he continued as a publisher until the college closed in 1956, which, as it happens, was the year in which he brought out *The Improved Binoculars*.

The conventional wisdom of Canadian literary history has had it for some time that the appearance of *The Improved Binoculars* under an American imprint and with the impressive advantage of a William Carlos Williams endorsement is to be seen as an event of major consequence for Canadian poetry at the mid-century mark.

TIBBY, as Layton would come to call it in abbreviated form, began as an idea for a selected poems which Layton proposed to Jonathan Williams in a letter dated 13 October 1955, describing the project as something 'closer to my heart',[3] and prompted, he explained, by the fact that, 'Most of my earlier volumes are already out of print and unavailable'. He went on to suggest that the collection comprising some sixty 'choice' poems be called 'A Selection of Poems', and he offered to help pay for it with a contribution of two hundred (later increased to two hundred and fifty) dollars for an edition of five hundred copies. Williams was expected to keep three hundred copies and Layton would get the balance for his own distribution. At the same time, Layton was busy trying to arrange for a patron[4] for his manuscript, and to find a Canadian co-publisher to take on the project. On the 5th of December 1955, he wrote to Williams to report that Lorne Pierce of Ryerson Press had agreed to become a partner in the undertaking. A buoyed-up Layton reported to Robert Creeley on the 16th,

---

[3] It would appear that the correspondence between Layton and Jonathan Williams had been interrupted and Layton, who had assembled his manuscript of *The Bull Calf and Other Poems* with the intention of submitting it to Williams, had dispatched it instead with Gael Turnbull who had set off for England in the hope that he would find a publisher for it there. Turnbull was not successful and the book appeared under the Contact Press imprint in 1956. Clearly, Layton had set his heart on a selection of his better poems, those '... known and liked by a fairly large audience'.

[4] Francis Mansbridge in his note in *Wild Gooseberries: The Selected Letters of Irving Layton* (Toronto: Macmillan, 1989) to Layton's letter

'Have been up to my neck with TIBBY, answering letters of J[onathan] W[illiams] and the publisher who's also coming in on this, Ryerson Press. It's all fixed now. RP have agreed to take 200 copies which you may be certain is a relief to both me & brother Jonathan.' (*The Complete Correspondence*, 245)

This happy state of affairs was not to last however, for Ryerson Press, stunned by the explicit language[5] in some of Layton's poems, backed out of its commitment.[6]

---

to Jonathan Williams of 4 December 1955 says that Layton had been led to believe that help would be forthcoming to make it possible for him to publish a new collection of poems.

[5] The source of angst for a publishing house which had been founded by the Methodist Church appears to have been (as Layton reported to Williams a year later on the 22nd of December 1956) Layton's reference to 'the blood and balls of Christ' in his poem, 'The Poetic Process', and what he described as 'some of the erotica in the book'.

Layton was annoyed at Canadian publishers, 'God rot their souls' he said in the same letter, although he was not insensitive to the discomfort such a reference might engender in a Christian sensibility. For example, in discussing his poems for possible inclusion in A.J.M. Smith's *The Book of Canadian Poetry* (1957) and in *The Blasted Pine* (1957), Layton offered to replace 'balls' with 'bones', and he appears to have offered the same option to Williams, although on 3 June 1956 he had a change of mind and insisted (with capital emphasis): 'WILL YOU PLEASE LEAVE THE ORIGINAL "balls"'. Three years later in *A Red Carpet for the Sun* an even more significant collection and one with which Layton would take the Governor General's Award for poetry and seize the attention of Canadian critics and public alike, 'balls' had been changed to 'gall'. Layton's intention as to the latter word's meaning is not clear.

[6] In his letter to Robert Creeley of the 26th of January 1957, Layton offered the following account of his problems with Ryerson Press:

The other bit of drama (and it was no mean thing) attending the arrangements leading up to the publication of TIBBY was the two-page introduction, 'A Note on Layton', penned by the great eminence of modern poetry, William Carlos Williams, and containing the now famous sentence, 'When I first clapped eyes on the poems of Irving Layton, two years ago, I let out a yell of joy.' Undeniably this was a great coup and a great boost for Layton's morale, he who had just written to Creeley in his typical and embattled fashion,

> 'No man gives less of a fuck as to what any of the benighted tribe of crappers have to say abt [sic] my poetry or anyone else's.' (*The Complete Correspondence*, 245)

A little more than a month later, on the 26th of January 1956, Layton would open his letter to Jonathan Williams with,

> 'The news from Wm C Wms made me kick my heels in the air. I can't say I've come down yet.' (*Wild Gooseberries*, 66)

The euphoria was genuine, and the event a momentous one for Layton. Elspeth Cameron, writing years later as his biographer,

---

'You may have heard that the Canadian publisher, RYERSON Press, which contracted to distribute the book in this country, now flatly say they are not going to do so. At the present they are sitting on a cargo of 200 copies; and the office lady in charge spits out at any one who asks that not a single copy will leave their hallowed precincts. I say "hallowed" advisedly for RP is the publishing arm of The United Church. It seems that one of my poems hints that Christ may have had BALLS and that such a frightening thought had never entered the scrubbed minds of the assorted crew cuts and clerical collars who form the committee on book publications.' (*The Complete Correspondence*, 251)

would link this moment to the emotional intensity that Layton's life began to display at that time. She described it thus,

'William Carlos Williams to whom the manuscript for *The Improved Binoculars* had been sent, responded in superlatives: "You have one of the major talents of the age, I only wish I were half as good."' (*Irving Layton: A Portrait*, 270)

She would also go on to say that in Louis Dudek's opinion,

'Layton changed dramatically when he gained the attention of the American poets Williams, Creeley, Olson and Corman.' (*Irving Layton: A Portrait*, 272)

Dudek's point is an interesting one because it raises the question of Layton's relationship to Contact Press, that key venture of inspired cooperative publishing which provided Canadian poetry with its most important impetus at a critical time in the development of a modern idiom in Canadian poetics. Significantly, of the triumvirate (after all had they not chosen the name of Cerberus the three-headed dog of mythology for their joint, first title of Contact Press) it was Layton who carved the most independent path for himself and achieved the most visible achievement in terms of his career. No small measure of this success was due to the relationship that grew out of a link-up – in various ways – with a group of emerging but not particularly well-known or established American poets now loosely termed the Black Mountain Group with whom Layton established an unusual rapport. One says unusual because, if anything, it is Layton's poetry with its fiery rhetoric, its declamatory qualities, and its strong and overtly expressed sentiments that had least in common with the laconic densities, the introversions and the tight verbal spirals of the Cormans, the Creeleys and the Olsons. Equally paradoxical is the fact that while it was Dudek who had first established contact with Cid Corman and who had brought the group's activities to the attention of Souster and Layton, it would also be Dudek who would have least to do with these American contacts. At the same time Cid Corman became a grey presence in the background of Raymond Souster's magazine *Contact*, and Robert Creeley became Layton's faithful correspondent, arranger of books[7] and maker of contacts. Cid Corman, too, had a significant role to play chiefly through the medium of his avant-garde magazine, *Origin* (1st Series).[8] He wrote Raymond Souster from Paris on the 3rd of March 1955 to say: '#14 [of *Origin*] is really Irving's show and he does look damned good. And I have an equally large group of things from him, at least as good, to come –', and in the next letter of the 21st of March 1955 he would say,

'Glad #14 finally reached you and that it makes it altogether. The comments have varied some, though largely very favorable. One or two have felt that Irving is very uneven. And his story has received comment from

---

[7] For example, beginning with Layton's *In the Midst of my Fever* (1954) the publication of which Creeley engineered under the imprint of The Divers Press when he was living in Palma de Mallorca and for which, incidentally, Jonathan Williams designed the cover, and following through with *The Blue Propeller* (1955), Creeley worked as a kind of 'fixer' (in the best sense of the word) for Layton's international contacts. It was also Creeley who brought Layton onto the editorial board of the newly-founded *Black Mountain Review* where, in 1954, he joined Paul Blackburn, Charles Olson and Kenneth Patchen on the masthead as one of the contributing editors. *Black Mountain Review* has been recently described by Ekbert Faas and Sabrina Reed in their Introduction to the Layton / Creeley correspondence as 'one of the major organs of early "Postmodernism in America"'.

[8] Cid Corman featured Layton in his magazine and had him guest-edit an issue devoted to Canadian poetry.

one extreme to the other. I dont as readily go off the deep end. I think some of his work in #14 as good as any *he* has done. And in Canada that is almost synonymous with the best Canadian poetry. Now if he would stop feeling as though he was and had to be the best in the country, he might develop more. Something, too often, provincial. Defensive. But beyond all such, he is capable of very strong poems and a good strong use of language.'

The importance of these early American contacts in the initial surge of Layton's career in the nineteen fifties cannot be underestimated, and his own letters of the period are as peppered with uncomplimentary remarks about Canadian critics as they are laced with disdain for the Canadian literary establishment. As he said in his letter to Jonathan Williams acknowledging words of praise and news of William Carlos Williams' introduction for *The Improved Binoculars*:

'How different a poet going the the heart of the matter from the Canadian frosty faces. So often I wish the critics would simply drop dead. Even their most perceptive remarks strike me as being most of the time quite irrelevant. I call them simply castratos.' (*Wild Gooseberries*, 66)

Sixteen years later, mellowed by success and reassured by the knowledge that he had achieved great prominence as a Canadian poet, Layton would still hold to the view that,

'He [Robert Creeley] was the only one, and it's significant that he was an American, who felt that my work was valuable enough to be published.' (L.J. Resnitzky, 'An Interview with Irving Layton', *Le Chien d'Or / The Golden Dog*. No. 1, January 1972)

In this belief Layton has remained remarkably consistent and would continue to insist eighteen years later that,

'I think the main point to be stressed is the reception the
Americans gave my work in contrast to that of the
carping, mean-spirited Canadians.' (Layton to
Gnarowski, 22 June 1990)

The longer view now suggests that the 'American' phase of
Layton's career in which *The Improved Binoculars* is a landmark
collection, was of major importance in establishing him as a
poet of standing. It is not only that TIBBY sold well enough in
its first printing that a second edition would soon be indicated,
but that the connection with Jonathan Williams would lead to
another collection, *A Laughter in the Mind* which Williams
would publish in 1958 as *Jargon 28*, and which was also
destined to go into a second edition in 1959 under the imprint
of Editions d'Orphée of Montreal with twenty additional
poems. All of this, it could be argued, led to *A Red Carpet for
the Sun* and the Governor General's Award the next year.

After TIBBY's publication and release late in 1956, there was
one more moment of drama and excitement arising out of the
ill-advised decision of Ryerson Press to 'suppress' the book. As
Layton had reported gleefully to Robert Creeley, Ryerson's
receptionist had informed all and sundry that not one copy of
the book would leave their premises. On the 11th of January he
wrote to Jonathan Williams with even greater satisfaction that,

'Attendez! Attendez! Something very especially good is
about to break for our tribe. Anne Wilkinson, Toronto
scribe, attractive and friendly, just phoned me long
distance to tell me that a big story is about to break in the
Toronto Globe & Mail. That's one of Canada's most
influential papers, our *London Times*, the sheet most
frequently found at ministers' elbows. And what's the
story? That Ryerson Press won't release the copies of
TIBBY but intends to stack them away in their warehouse
where the rats can get at them.' (*Wild Gooseberries*, 80)

And then again, a little later that month,

> 'Almost every day, orders are coming in for the book.
> Yesterday I received a letter from a representative of an
> engineers' & chemists' group way up in Shawinigan Falls,
> Que., saying she wanted to place an order for several
> copies. The group had decided that if my bk was being so
> treated, it must be worth careful study.' (*Wild
> Gooseberries*, 81)

Buoyed by the sense that he was becoming something of a
celebrity, Layton cast about for an alternative to Ryerson Press
and approached Jack McClelland in the hope that the latter
would make *The Improved Binoculars* part of McClelland &
Stewart's Indian File Series[9] only to be turned down by the
very same people who, two years later, would be instrumental
in launching and promoting him on his spectacular career in
Canadian poetry.

What the Thundering Critics Said ...

From 1945 when Layton published his first book he had
been developing an outspoken antipathy for critics and
reviewers, and when *The Improved Binoculars* appeared this
skirmishing had become a trademark of Layton's relationship
with the literary press. Both in his private communications
where he was inclined to be sulphurous and scatological, and
in his public responses to his critics, Layton maintained a
fighting posture which demanded that they pay serious

---

9 McClelland & Stewart's Indian File Series was a sedately-designed
(Layton described the covers as 'ghastly coffin boards') series of
books of poetry by the new or newer poets of the fifties. Of its first
nine titles, three won the Governor General's Award. James Reaney,
Patrick Anderson, P.K. Page, Phyllis Webb and John Glassco
appeared in the Series.

attention to what he was saying in his poetry and the manner in which he was doing it. For example, when TIBBY was in its final stages of production Layton was engaged in an active campaign to persuade A.J.M. Smith, then at the peak of his influence as critic and anthologist, to show more understanding and receptivity[10] to Layton's kind of poetry. There was banter and insouciance in the letters that they exchanged, but there was also an underlying seriousness and conviction on Layton's part which Smith could not misunderstand.

Browsing through those reviews of 1957 one senses that Layton had succeeded in making his point. Even the stodgy inanities in which the *Times Literary Supplement* cloaked its remarks – it could not resist picking up on William Carlos Williams' reference to Layton as a backwoodsman – contained the observation that 'At his best, he has at his command a sweet and unforced vein of lyricism, and there is nothing unpleasing in the frank sensuality of many of his love poems.' Kildare Dobbs harrumphed in his review in the *Canadian Forum* but had to grant that Layton's best poems were those in which 'he forgets to be a Poet and is possessed by the poem instead, and sings', while Northrop Frye who wrinkled his nose at the 'backwoodsman' epithet, said, quite generously, that 'The collection is strongly recommended to those who are becoming curious about this poet....' For Norman Endicott writing his 'Poetry Chronicle' in the *Tamarack Review*, Layton was someone who 'sees more clearly the ugly, the stupid, and the brutally callous in the social life of his city'. He then went

---

[10] Smith was a late convert to Layton's poetry. He had managed to leave Layton out of the first and second editions of his influential anthology, *The Book of Canadian Poetry* (1943 & 1948), and began to come around slowly in the mid-1950s. His 'conversion' which he tried to explain (lamely) in his article, 'The Recent Poetry of Irving Layton' in *Queens Quarterly* in the winter of 1956 was roundly derided by Louis Dudek who responded with his own piece, 'Layton Now and Then' in the following issue of the journal.

on to say (enigmatically ?) that 'Since he is a defeated individual of integrity and energy he is a writer to be glad of in any day and especially in our boom times.'

The most significant discussion of *The Improved Binoculars*, however, in terms of Layton's international reputation, occurred in *Poetry* (Chicago). In an omnibus review which included Olson's *Maximus 11/22* sequence and Ginsberg's *Howl*, Frederick Eckman identified Layton as one of the 'genuine wild men in the best little magazine tradition', and then went on to praise him for his 'savage wit', his 'erotic preoccupations' and 'the frequent unevenness of an e.e. cummings'.

Not unexpectedly, and especially because Layton had chosen to advertise his debt to D.H. Lawrence and to Nietzsche and Marx on the inside flap of the cover, critics attempted to tie his eroticism to Lawrence and his politics to Marx. This seemed an easier thing to do than to recognise what has now become obvious: Layton's 'vitality', 'gaiety', 'lyricism' were less a product of his reading than they were an extension of his poetic persona and his direct and disputatious self. An outsider and a maverick in what John Sutherland had described aptly as 'the closed chamber of Canadian letters', Layton offered his readers a selection of hard-fisted poems which would become a serious and enduring part of the general clamour that he had set up. Many of these poems – after all Layton had labelled them 'choice' – would find their way quietly and persuasively into anthologies, classrooms and public readings. There they would take their own places.

Michael Gnarowski

CONTENTS